The next 40 days can change your life!

One Goal:
To have a more intimate relationship
with God

A Simple Plan:
To keep a daily appointment to be still
and know that He is God.

Shhh...

Be Still and Know

A Prayer Journal for the
Not-So-Super Saint

By

James E. Hollars

Taylor Jewel Press
P. O. Box 100126
Fort Worth, TX 76185

Published in Fort Worth, Texas by Taylor Jewel Press.

Scripture quotations marked (NLT) are taken from the *Holy Bible, New Living Translation,* copyright © 1996. Used by permission of Tyndale House Publishers, Inc., Wheaton, Illinois 60189. All rights reserved.

Scripture quotations marked (NIV) are taken from the *Holy Bible, New International Version,* copyright ©1973, 1978, 1984 by International Bible Society. Used by permission of International Bible Society.

The scripture quotation marked (NKJV) is from *The New King James Bible,* copyright ©1982 by Thomas Nelson, Inc.

The scripture quotation marked (TEV) is from *The Bible in Today's English Version,* copyright © American Bible Society, 1976.

The scripture quotation marked (TLB) is from *The Living Bible* (TLB) copyright © 1971 by Tyndale House Publishers, Wheaton, Illinois 60187. All rights reserved.

ISBN: 978-0-9792941-0-5

Editors: Cynthia Ives, Deborah Sneed

Cover Photography and Design: Heather Essian

Dedication

To

Pastor Shane Gray
Hope Works Fellowship,
Fort Worth, Texas

Pastor Gray's enthusiasm for the potential of this prayer journal encouraged me to retrieve a half-finished manuscript from the inactive files.

His belief that his congregation could profit from using the prayer journal moved it into the active files.

His continuing encouragement during the long process of putting it all together pushed us through re-write after re-write until the day we sent the PDF file to the printer.

Author Information

Jim Hollars grew up in a Christian home in Vernon and Lubbock, Texas and came to know Christ at an early age. He graduated from Texas Tech (1964) and Southwestern Baptist Theological Seminary (1992), and served churches in Texas and Ohio as a music and youth minister for 30 years and as a pastor for 14 years.

He is associated with Baseball Chapel, an evangelistic and discipleship ministry to professional baseball. He was assistant Chapel Leader for the Toledo Mud Hens for three seasons and has been Chapel Leader for the Fort Worth Cats since 2002.

He has been married to Shirley since 1975. They have five daughters, seven granddaughters, one grand son, and 5 sons-in-law. Jim and Shirley are members of Christ Chapel Bible Church in Fort Worth.

Contact Information

James E. Hollars
PO Box 100126
Fort Worth, TX 76185
(817) 346-1387
hollars@sbcglobal.net

Table of Contents

Come and Go With Me

My favorite music video is Audio Adrenalin's *Big House*, an exuberant song about Heaven as a teenager or twenty-something might see it. The chorus is an invitation—a contagious tune that keeps replaying over and over in my mind:

Come and go with me to my Father's house

This prayer journal, with its personal stories, is written as that kind of invitation:
Come and go with me.

I am a chronic type-A, living life on the run, moving from activity to activity, judging my day by the number of check marks on my "to do" list. Yet, for several years God has allowed me to experience daily fellowship with Him that involves being still and loving it—looking forward to it as the best time of the day.

This prayer journal, with its personal stories,

is written as that kind of invitation:

Come and go with me.

If you already have a daily time like that, you know what I am talking about. If you don't, this prayer journal is my invitation for you to *come and go with me* on a 40-day quest of a daily fellowship with God. I believe it can be your best time of the day, too.

Each day will be built around a borrowed prayer from the Bible. Read its context in the Bible, meditate on the scripture prayer, use it in conversation with God, and jot some notes about its impact. We will do that in a few minutes, set aside each day to
Shhh . . . be still and know

Shhh...

Shhh…

Be still…

Listen…

Be still, and know that I am God…

Shhh…

I sat on the couch in the pre-dawn darkness in our living room in Toledo, Ohio, sipping a fresh-brewed cup of coffee. It was my favorite time of the day and my favorite place to enjoy it. No matter what happened the day before or what loomed ahead, it all had a different perspective in this unhurried early morning fellowship with God.

In the quietness before the world began to wake up for another day, I cherished my time alone with God in our living room. No matter what happened the day before or what loomed ahead, it all had a different perspective in this unhurried early morning fellowship with God.

I had some things I wanted to talk with the Lord about, some requests to make - but He would not let me begin.

Shhh…

Listen…

Be still, and know that I am God.

It was not a harsh rebuke, but a gentle invitation.

Daylight was an hour or so away as I sipped my coffee and enjoyed my time with God. The rest of the world appeared to be

2

asleep, but I was awake and God was there. Later, the clock and the day's checklist might tyrannize me, but for now, there was no hurry.

Eventually, I would turn the lights on in the kitchen, refill my coffee cup, and continue this time with God by sitting down at the dining room table to read from His Word.

I desperately needed that time with Him. The dream of my life, planting a church to reach people who did not know Jesus personally, had become an overwhelming task.

The dream had its genesis years ago at a summer camp near Vernon, Texas - a thousand miles from Toledo. I told a counselor that God wanted me to be a missionary. I was eleven years old. To this day I remember how strong that call was. It was something I had to do.

In my early 30's, that call led me to leave the Bible Belt to help smaller churches in the North – first as a minister of music and youth and then as a pastor.

In 1990, I was asked about starting a church in Toledo to reach unchurched people with the Gospel. That conversation was a spark that ignited a fire in my heart to do just that.

Starting that church was one of the joys of my life,

but that joy was wearing me out.

That call was as intense as any I had ever known. By late 1994 all the pieces had fallen in place, and the first Sunday in December seven people met in a home to talk and pray about starting a church. Six months later we had the first public worship service of Gateway Community Church.

I poured my life into Gateway. I loved that church. I loved the people we were reaching. Many knew very little about the Lord in the beginning and even less about "doing church."

From the first, we seemed to attract hurting people; hurting people that we could love to Jesus. We saw God working in people. We saw people come to know Jesus. We saw hurts healed.

3

But not all the hurts. I had read, "Hurt people hurt people". That was true at Gateway. Our people brought baggage with them that they had to be taught to throw away. Combined with the overwhelming task of organizing a church from scratch and the long hours it took to prepare sermons that would speak to people who normally did not listen to sermons, I was a living recipe for exhaustion. Starting that church was one of the joys of my life, but that joy was wearing me out.

That was the situation as I sat on the couch in the dark living room with my cup of coffee. The situation was urgent. I wanted to get right to my requests, but God would not let me begin.

Be still, and know that I am God.

Shhh…

Be still…

Be still, and know that I am God.

It was as if God was quietly, gently saying, "Don't talk. Listen."

Instead of plunging into my prayer list, I thought about what it meant to be still. I saw the need to wait patiently for God's Spirit to direct this prayer time. I thought about what it means to know that He is God—how that affects the way I live, the way I think.

All hurry was gone. I could just enjoy this time with Him.

It was the same way the next morning. There would be plenty of time to pray about all our needs, but He wanted me to listen first. And I had to learn to be still before I could learn to listen.

In the stillness I remembered again that He is in charge. He knows where I am. He called me to this ministry. Those mornings became times of communion with Him when He would remind me of scripture that spoke to my concerns of the moment.

God still has to remind me today. Some mornings our time together begins with:

Shhh…

Be still, and know that I am God. I will be exalted on the earth.

4

The prayers we will borrow do not exist in a vacuum; they are all part of the Bible story. Knowing something about how the prayer fits in God's word will add to your understanding and use of the prayer. Therefore, each of the forty prayers used in this journal will have a brief summary of its context.

Context
    God responds to a psalmist's list of His attributes.

Read
Psalm 46: 1-11

Your response may be, "Wait a minute. This is not a prayer we can say to God; it is God talking to us."

It is God speaking, but remember

Prayer Is A Two-Way Conversation.

A monologue is not conversation. If we do all the talking we will miss God's contribution to our talk. Always think of prayer as a two-way conversation between God and you. Listen to Him. Respond to Him.

After you read the Bible passage each day, take time to meditate — to think about the scripture.

Meditate
    Think about the prayer; ask questions; take your time.

Relax. Be still. Think about the idea of being still. How difficult is that for you? Suppress any sense of urgency. This is your time with God. What an awesome thought! Don't let anything interfere with this moment. Notice that the purpose of this time is not just to be still; it is to be still and know that He Is God. Think about how a daily time to be quiet and to know once again that He is in charge will affect you. The scripture goes on to say that He will be exalted. All honor and glory are His.

Note: See more on meditation on page 68.

Meditation should flow easily and naturally
into the next step: prayer.

Pray

_____

Be still, and know that I am God;
Psalm 46:10 (NIV)

_____

If you are not sure how to engage God in conversational prayer, here are some suggestions for the first day.

Tell God you are ready to listen. Ask Him to direct this time together. Ask Him to open your mind to the truths in the scripture you have just read. Ask Him what it means to "be still" in your relationship with Him. How can you be still in His presence? Listen. Be still. Push aside today's "to do" list. Shelve problems or challenges you are facing. There will be time for all of that later. Rest in the security of His presence. Find peace in the reality that He loves you. Think about who He is. Tell Him you would like to know Him more intimately and you are willing to listen in order to do that. Listen. Be still. Thank Him for your time together.

Notes
Write your thoughts and your experiences with today's prayer.

_____

_____

_____

_____

_____

_____

_____

_____

_____

Date_____

One of the first steps toward enjoying an intimate relationship with Almighty God is being sure of your relationship with Him. The first five days of this prayer journal are designed to help you nail down the assurance that you know God personally through a saving relationship with the Lord Jesus Christ.

As you read today's borrowed prayer, spend some time thinking about Paul's question and Jesus' answer as well as the discussion Jesus had with His disciples in **Luke 9:18-24**. Then talk with Him in prayer about who He is.

Context
> Paul the Apostle tells the story of his conversion from an enemy of Christ to an evangelist for His message. He told about being struck down by a vision of the Lord Jesus. He asked Jesus who He was. He addressed Him as Lord—recognition that this Christ had his complete allegiance.

Read
> **Acts 26: 4-18; Luke 9:18 -24**

Meditate
> Think about the prayer, ask questions, and take your time.

Pray

Who are you, Lord?
Acts 26:15 (NIV)

Notes

_____

_____

_____

_____

_____

Day 3   Date _____

Context
>   The Jews kept turning their backs on God despite His warnings
>   of dire consequences. Finally he allowed them to be
>   conquered and many of their leaders taken as exiles to
>   Babylon. The exile got their attention. Now, He would bring
>   them home, just as He had promised. This scripture passage is
>   a letter to them, but its
>   promises are universal to all
>   who worship Him as the Lord
>   of their life.

Read
>   **Jeremiah 29:1-14**

Meditate

Pray

If possible, set aside the
same time in the same
place every day for this
prayer journal. Reserve
that time as your first
priority of each day.

_____

You will seek me and find me
when you seek me with all your heart
Jeremiah 29:13 (NIV)

_____

Notes

_____

_____

_____

_____

_____

_____

_____

_____

How do you see yourself before God?

Do you recognize that your sin has separated you from Him and that you need His mercy? Unless you realize that salvation is a gift you cannot earn, you are in the same category as the first man in Jesus' story. To know God, you must have the heart of the second man who recognized his need for forgiveness and cried out, "God be merciful to me a sinner."

Context
    Jesus tells the story of two men who were praying. One bragged to God about the man he claimed to be, but was not. The other recognized that he was a sinner and cried out to God for mercy. Jesus said it was the second man, not the first, who went home in a right relationship with God.

Read
    Luke 18: 9-14

Depending on your relationship with Jesus, this prayer could either be a thanksgiving or an appeal.

Meditate
    If you are NOT
    sure of your
    relationship with
    Jesus Christ
today's meditation, prayer, and journaling time can help you take the steps to nail it down.

If you ARE sure of your relationship with Jesus Christ today's meditation, prayer, and journaling time can be the opportunity to talk with Him about that assurance and to thank Him for it.

Pray

_____

God be merciful to me a sinner.
Luke 18:13 (KJV)

_____

Notes

_____

_____

_____

Context
> Jesus appeared to His followers after He was resurrected from the dead, but Thomas, was not present. He did not believe when the others told him and said he would not believe unless certain conditions were met. When he saw Jesus for himself, he forgot all about his conditions and immediately worshipped Christ as "my Lord and my God."

Read
John 20: 19-29

Jesus said He is God. Some people say He was a good man or a great teacher, but that He was not God. The late Oxford professor C. S. Lewis said one has an insurmountable intellectual problem if he or she says Jesus was a good man, but was not God. He says that choice is not left open to us because Jesus said He is God.

Lewis says if Jesus thought He was God and He was not, that makes Him a lunatic. If He knew He was not God, but said He was that makes Him a liar. How can you give much credence to the actions or teachings of a liar or a lunatic?

Jesus was either a liar, a lunatic, or He is God. If He is God we need to obey Him as Lord and worship Him as God.

Meditate
> Have you found the answer? Who is Jesus?
> If Jesus is your Lord, your God, what are the implications for your life?

Pray

_____

My LORD and my God.
John 20:28 (KJV)

_____

Notes

_____

_____

_____

Day 6   Date_____

Context
> This psalm begins with a majestic proclamation of God's power, affirms how that power protects His people, and ends with a statement of confidence that God's goodness will endure.

Read
> **Psalm 27:1-14**

Did you notice verse 8?

> Incredible. This great and mighty, all-powerful God invites us to "come and talk with me." We don't seek out God and try to convince Him to spend a few minutes listening to our appeals. No. He invites us. You are on this quest at His invitation.

Meditate

Pray

_____

My heart has heard you say,
"Come and talk with me."
And my heart responds, "LORD, I am coming."
Psalm 27:8 (NLT)

_____

Notes

_____

_____

_____

_____

11

Context

Hagar, a pregnant slave girl, ran away to escape the severe abuse of her jealous mistress. An angel sent her back home with the promise that God would take care of her and the son she was bearing. Forever after, Hagar referred to the Lord as "The God who sees me."

Read

Genesis 16: 1-16

Meditate

Pray

_____

**You are the God who sees me.
Genesis 16:13 (NIV)**

_____

Notes

_____

_____

_____

_____

_____

_____

_____

Years ago my friend Eldon King decided that he needed to get up early every morning to pray. He set his alarm. When it went off, he got out of bed, got on his knees, and began to pray. He promptly went back to sleep on his knees.

That discouraged him, but he tried it again the next morning. His alarm went off; he got out of bed, got on his knees, and began to pray. Again, almost instantly, he went back to sleep.

"This is not working," he thought. But morning after morning, he kept setting his alarm. It took a while, but he was eventually able to stay awake. His early-morning prayer time became a habit. He began to look forward to that early morning appointment with God.

Weekly Reflection

You now have at least seven prayers in your vocabulary. Take a few minutes to review them.

Which prayer has had the most impact on your relationship with God so far?

Have you found yourself using any of the prayers in conversations with God throughout the day?

Have any of the prayers come on "just the right day?" That will happen occasionally and leave you amazed at God's timing.

Always think of prayer as a
two-way conversation
between God and you.
Listen to Him.
Respond to Him.

Context
> The disciples observed Jesus in prayer and asked Him to teach them to pray. He taught them what is popularly called "The Lord's Prayer".

Read
> **Luke 11:1-14**

Meditate
> What is your greatest desire in learning to pray?
> What do you think will happen if you prayed, "Lord, teach me to pray for the next 40 days?"

Pray

_____

Lord, teach us to pray
Luke 11:1 (NIV)

_____

Notes

_____

_____

_____

_____

What if you saw prayer as primarily about having a relationship with God? The Bible says we are to ask. That is certainly a part of what prayer is. But what if you saw prayer as far more than making requests? What affect would it have on the way you pray if you saw prayer as having more to do with an intimate relationship with God than it is about making requests?

Awestruck

I stood one morning on the rim of the Grand Canyon in northern Arizona astonished by its vastness. I had seen photographs of the canyon, but no picture could capture its enormity. My mind could not comprehend what my eyes were seeing. I was awestruck by what I saw.

A few years later I stood in a hospital room in Dayton, Ohio holding Courtney, our first grandchild, in my hands, staring at her in a wonder beyond any I had experienced. Perhaps when her mother was born twenty years earlier I had not been mature enough to grasp how incredible this new life was. I was awestruck by what I felt.

On a cold winter night three years later I joined several thousand excited people inside the warm Market Square Arena in Indianapolis. We were in the home of the Indiana Pacers, but we were not there to see a basketball game; we were there to hear a sound. It was a sound I had heard many times on recordings, but tonight I would hear it live.

Luciano Pavarotti, perhaps at the peak of his career, shared his gift with us that evening. He seemed almost in as much awe of the sound coming from his voice as we were. He had written once that God had kissed his vocal cords. I was awestruck by what I heard.

Recently I had an experience in the stillness of the night that also left me awestruck. I have periodic bouts with insomnia, so it is not unusual for me to be awake at that hour.

On this night, I was struggling. I had failed God—sinned is the upfront word. I had admitted that to God. I felt separated from Him. My relationship with Him had lost the joy, the peace He had shared with me recently. I missed that.

I lay in bed praying, trying to convince God that I would try harder, stay alert to temptation if only He would take me back to that place of fellowship I had enjoyed so much recently.

He would have none of it. There was no way I was going to earn my way back into His good graces.

Graces?

Grace!

That's what this was all about. Slowly I began to understand a truth I had talked about for years. I could never win His favor...but I had it. He had already given it to me through His grace.

This truth seemed to roll over me like a blanket of love that He placed over me. I was awestruck by His presence.

Date _____

Context

    The prophet Habakkuk questions why God does not save His people from injustice; why the wicked outnumber the righteous; why God was using the wicked Babylonians to punish and correct Israel. God answers him by reaffirming His sovereignty and the ultimate victory of justice. Habakkuk is awestruck when he considers God's ways.

Read

Habakkuk 2:14- 3:2

Habakkuk was awestruck as he thought of all that God had done.

Meditate

    Spend some time today thinking about all God is. Use your journal to begin making a list. Add to your list throughout the day. When you have finished, read them back to Him.

Pray

    _____

I am filled with awe
by the amazing things you have done.
Habakkuk 3:2 (NLT)

    _____

Notes

_____

_____

_____

_____

_____

_____

_____

Do you cringe when you hear God referred to as the "Man Upstairs"? How do you react when you hear Him called "The Big Guy?" Or when someone uses "Oh, my G...!" or a similar expression as an expletive?

Context
> The model prayer Jesus used to teach His disciples to pray begins with the recognition of the holiness of God's name.

God's very name is holy.

The scholars who produced the New American Standard Bible capitalize all pronouns that refer to God. Normally, pronouns are not capitalized in the English. The NASB insist that even a pronoun that represents a name of God is to be treated with respect – i.e., capitalized. It is poor grammar on the part of the NASB, but it is great theology.

Read
> **Luke 11:1-4**

Meditate
> Hallowed means to regard as holy or sacred. Think about how you apply that to God's name as you meditate and pray, "Father, hallowed be Your name."

Pray

_____

Father, hallowed be your name.
Luke 11:2 (NIV)

_____

Notes

_____

_____

_____

_____

_____

Search My Heart, O God

**Search me, O God, and know my heart. Try me and know my thoughts: and see if there be any wicked way in me.
Psalm 139:23-24 (KJV)**

The speaker at Richland Hills Baptist Church urged us to pray this prayer daily as a way of keeping "our sins forgiven up-to-date." He suggested asking God to show us any sins we had not repented of and to write them on a "sin list", keeping the list secret so we could be specific. When we finished the list, we were to work through it, truly repenting of each sin with the desire to never do it again. If another person was involved we should go to them, confess our sin against them, and ask their forgiveness.

**If we confess our sins, He is faithful and just, and will forgive us our sins and purify us from all unrighteousness.
John 1:9 (KJV)**

When we finished, we were to claim the promise of 1 John 1:9 for each sin, scratch that sin off of our list, thank God that the sin was gone forever, then destroy the list.

I decided to pray the prayer. I had an idea what would go on it. Was I in for a surprise! Almost immediately, the idea popped in my mind.

"You hate _____."

That shocked me. I did not hate anybody. I wanted to argue with God. (A great way to start a confession.) He would not let me off the hook. I had some differences with a man that I had suppressed. God answered my prayer by dragging the problem out into the light.

That man was the first of many people to whom I had to apologize. It was a painful, embarrassing exercise in obedience to God—but when I finished scratching off the last sin on that list and then destroyed the list, I WAS FREE!

Date _____

You have no secrets from God, but do you keep secrets from yourself? Do you have sin hidden away in some recess of your mind or heart? You put it there because you do not want to talk about or even think about it. You would really like to pretend it never happened. But it did. And unless you confess that sin and ask God's forgiveness, it is still there.

Context
    The psalmist recognizes that God knows everything about him. He concludes his song by asking God to open his eyes so he can see himself as God sees him.

Read
    Psalm 139: 1-18, 23-24

Meditate

Pray

Search me, O God, and know my heart. try me and know my thoughts: and see if there be any wicked way in me. Psalm 139:23-24 (KJV)

Notes
    Use a separate sheet of paper for today's notes so you can destroy it when you are finished.

1. Ask God to show you any sin in your life that you have not confessed and repented. Write them on the "sin list." Be specific.

2. If you have sinned against another person, admit your sin to them and ask their forgiveness. (See caution, p. 24)

3. Claiming the promise of 1 John 1:9 ask God to forgive you for each sin on your list. As you deal with each sin, scratch it off your list.

4. When you are finished, destroy the list. Rejoice in God's grace.

Day 12   Date _____

Context

> The Bible calls King David a man after God's own heart, yet
> along with the good in his heart, he could also be a great
> sinner. One of his greatest sins began with adultery and led
> to murder. When a prophet confronted him he admitted his
> guilt. Psalm 51 is his cry for forgiveness. It is the repentance of
> a broken man.

Read

Psalm 51:1-19

Psalm 139:23-24 called our attention to sin we had not confessed
and 1 John 1:9 to the promise of forgiveness for sin we do confess.
Today's prayer focuses on the source of that forgiveness: God's
unfailing love.

The prayer does not ask for mercy because we deserve it. It asks
for mercy based on His unfailing love. His mercy is a gift of love.
The New Testament uses the word grace. His mercy comes from
His amazing grace.

Meditate

Pray

_____

Have mercy upon me, O God,
according to your unfailing love.
Psalm 51:1 (NIV)

_____

Notes

_____

_____

_____

_____

_____

_____

21

Day 13   Date _____

Context
>   Psalm 119 has 176 verses, making it the longest psalm in the
>   Bible. Verse one is a thesis statement for the psalm. **Happy
>   are people of integrity who follow the law of the Lord.** (The
>   Bible) The remaining 175 verses support that thesis.

Read
>   **Psalm 119: 1, 121-136**

Does God speak to us today? If so, how? Henry Blackaby says in
Experiencing God that God speaks through the Bible, prayer,
circumstances, and the church. These four ways are so
intertwined that sometimes they can hardly be separated. Since
the Bible is one of the primary ways God speaks to us, it is good to
develop the habit of asking God to speak through His words
anytime we read it.

Meditate
>   Can you recall a time when you were conscious of God
>   speaking to you through scripture?

Pray

_____

**Guide my steps by your word,
so I will not be overcome by any evil.
Psalm 119:133 (NLT)**

_____

Notes

_____

_____

_____

_____

_____

_____

Day 14   Date _____

Context
   In Paul's letter to the Colossian church he assures them of his
   prayers for them.

This blessing is a reminder that we need to include others in our
prayer relationship with God.

How do you pray for others? Do you pray for their needs to be
met—healing, a job, a crisis resolved? Keep it up. We should pray
for needs like that. A blessing, however, takes it a step further; a
blessing often involves their walk with the Lord. It is our desire that
they will know Him better.

Read
   Colossians 1:1-14

Meditate

Pray

May _____ be filled with the knowledge of Your will through all spiritual wisdom and understanding.
Colossians 1:9 (personalized)

Notes
   Write down names of people for whom you want to pray

_____

_____

_____

_____

_____

_____

Weekly Reflection

You now have at least 14 prayers in your vocabulary. Take a few minutes to review them.

Which prayer has had the most impact on your relationship with God so far?

Have you found yourself using any of the prayers in conversations with God throughout the day?

Have any of the prayers come on "just the right day?" That will happen occasionally and leave you amazed at God's timing.

A WORD OF CAUTION: Getting things right with people we have sinned against is an important part of the process of getting things right with God. But there are times when confessing your sin to another person could be inappropriate—even painful. Illustration: a group of teenagers were convicted about the way they had been making fun of an elderly gentleman in their church. Ridiculing him behind his back had become a cruel sport in the youth group. Several of them confessed this to him and asked his forgiveness. He had not known about their mocking him and was devastated by their confessions. If in doubt, ask God for wisdom.

Day 15   Date_____

Context
    The disciples observed Jesus in prayer and asked Him to
teach them to pray. He taught them what is popularly called
"The Lord's Prayer". Jesus included asking forgiveness in the
model prayer. Notice that he tied our asking forgiveness for
ourselves to our forgiving those who have sinned against us.

Read
Luke 11:1-14

> Do you struggle with forgiving those who have sinned against
> you? To refuse to forgive someone is an act of disobedience.

Meditate

Pray

_____

Forgive us our sins-- just as we
forgive those who have sinned against us.
Luke 11:4 (NLT)

_____

Notes
    Don't skip over this crucial step of forgiving those who have
sinned against you. Ask God about making a list of people
you have not forgiven. Delete their names as you forgive
them.

_____

_____

_____

_____

_____

Did you make a list of people you have not forgiven? What are
you going to do with the list?

25

Date_____

Satan's tactics for destroying people are countless--illegal drug use, greed, sex outside of marriage, divorce, abortion, homosexuality, hatred, and refusal to forgive. The result is ugly. The contrast between his ways and the Kingdom of God could not be greater. God's Kingdom is built on grace, love, fellowship, joy, and worshipping Him as Lord. In His Kingdom we will love Him and love others. And they will love us. Why would anyone ever choose Satan's ways?

Context
> Jesus gave "The Lord's Prayer", as it is popularly called, in answer to the disciples' request that He teach them to pray. He also included the prayer in His *Sermon on the Mount.*

Read
> **Matthew 6:8 -15**

Meditate
> Do you long for that day? We get glimpses of it when we let Him control our life, when we practice Kingdom living here and now. How can we do that consistently? We can pray for His Kingdom to have control in our life and in the hearts of others, as well.

Pray

_____

Your kingdom come, your will be done.
Matthew 6:10 (NIV)

_____

Notes

_____

_____

_____

_____

_____

The pop opera "Jesus Christ, Super Star" rocked many American churches when it crossed the Atlantic from Great Britain just six years behind the *Beatles*. Christian groups appalled by the coupling of rock music with Jesus' story attacked the rock music.

They should have been concerned about the text. Opinions about the music were based on taste, but the text was blasphemous. The opera's depiction of Jesus' prayer in Gethsemane was especially appalling. In *Jesus Christ, Super Star* Jesus complains that God holds all the cards, and while he agrees to go to the cross, he reminds God to hurry before he changes his mind. That cynical submission is not the Jesus of the Bible.

Context
>Jesus agonizes in the Garden of Gethsemane as the cross nears.

Read
>**Luke 22: 39-46**

Meditate
>Are you struggling with submission to God's will in a specific area?
>Talk to Him about it.

Pray

Not my will, but thine be done.
Luke 22:42 (KJV)

Notes

_____

_____

_____

_____

_____

David was a man who wanted to please God. A few minutes
strolling around on the roof of his palace, however, led to an
impulsive leap into sin that left him pleading with God to give him a
new heart. Walking on rooftops does not pose a problem for most
of us today, but a few minutes scrolling the Internet can expose us
to dangers David never faced. Today some men fall into the
clutches of pornography that creeps into their home on a
computer monitor. Other people battle drugs, alcohol, anger,
bitterness, dishonesty or over-eating. Their lives are out of control.
Unless God changes their inner most being, their behavior will
destroy them.

"Create in me a clean heart, O God" is not the intellectual request
of a rational person. It is the desperate cry of someone
overwhelmed by sin they cannot control.

Context
    David not only admits his guilt in his affair with Bathsheba, he
    pleads for God to change him.

Read
    Psalm 51:1-19

Meditate
    What do you want God to change in your life?
Pray

_____

Create in me a clean heart, O God.
Psalm 51:10 (KJV)

Notes

_____

_____

_____

_____

_____

_____

God, Please Change Me.
I Cannot Change Myself.

Billy Jack Dunlap was my friend, but he had had it with me. I was the wild man of the Tahoka Softball League and he was sick of watching my behavior. We played fast-pitch softball and I played it with an intensity that often led to my flying into a rage at umpires, opponents, or teammates.

After one of my blow-ups, Billy Jack said he wanted to talk to me. I told him I was going home.

"Sit down!" he demanded in such a way that I sat down. He said my behavior had to change immediately. "You say all those nice things at church on Sunday, and then you come down here and act worse than any player in the league during the week."

At first I got angry with Billy Jack, and then I began to defend myself. "I can't help it. I have tried to control my temper."

He would not back down. "You'd better find a way. You are doing more damage in our town than good. If you cannot control your temper, I wish you would leave."

That hurt, but I knew he was right. I was already praying about my temper. I prayed before every game, "God, I promise You I will not lose my temper tonight." My intentions were good, but I could not change.

God used that confrontation to teach me a lesson about prayer. I was desperate. I stopped telling God I was going to change. Instead I cried out, "God, I cannot control my temper. Please change me."

The summer was almost over and I had all winter to pray before a new season began the next spring. I pleaded with God to do something in me that I could not do for myself. I went to the first game of the next spring still asking God to change me. My first at bat a pitch came in high. Umpire Joe Brooks, a man I had had a run-in with the season before called it a strike. I turned and smiled at him.

He said, "What's the matter, Hollars? Didn't you like that call"?

I said, "Joe, if you called it a strike, it must have been a strike."

29

Incredulous, Joe ripped off his umpire's mask and bellowed to the crowd, "Did you hear what he said!"

After a couple of games people began to ask what happened. I told them that Billy Jack Dunlap was friend enough to confront me and God was big enough to change me.

I learned some lessons from that prayer of repentance that apply to every area of my life. (1) I admitted my sin, (2) I wanted desperately to change, but (3) realized I could not. (4) I asked God to change me. (5) He took my desire, added His power, and changed me.

Looking back, I realize He first changed my heart and my attitude toward the other players and the game itself. From that came the change in behavior.

Temptation would be easier to deal with if it did not catch me off guard so much. I keep getting blindsided by situations I did not anticipate.

What about a preemptive strike? Sometimes in struggling with temptation I have realized that I did not want to resist. I wanted to give in. Could I be honest and tell God that?

That honestly enables me to ask, "God, please change my "want to." My experience is He will answer that prayer.

Context
 The disciples observed Jesus in prayer and asked Him to teach them to pray. He taught them what is popularly called "The Lord's Prayer".

Read
 Luke 11: 1-13

Meditate
 Does God need to change your "want to" as the first step in your plea for a clean heart? What "want to" do you want God to change? Be specific.

Pray

_____

Don't let us yield to temptation.
Luke 11:4 (NLT)

_____

Notes

_____

_____

_____

_____

_____

_____

A woman named Hannah prayed earnestly for God to give her a child, promising to give him back to God for the rest of his days. God did. And she did. When Samuel was very young she took him to the tabernacle and gave him to Eli, the priest.

Context
> One night God called Samuel with a message for Eli.

Read
> **I Samuel 3: 1-19**

I remember this story from my childhood. Our teachers used color pictures, flannel graphs, and even a song to teach us the story of the little boy who finally realized it was God who was calling to him and said, "Speak, Lord. Your servant is listening."

Great story, but that is as far as they took it. They never told us that God had an unpleasant message He wanted Samuel to give his mentor Eli.

Meditate
> *What if God has a difficult or unpleasant message for you? Will you say, no matter what the assignment may be, "Speak, Lord, Your servant is listening."*

Pray

_____

Speak, LORD, your servant is listening.
I Samuel 3:9 (NIV)

_____

Notes

_____

_____

_____

_____

_____

Context
> A young prophet named Isaiah sees God in the temple and describes it with the skill of a master writer and the emotion of one remembering a once-in-a-lifetime experience.

Read
> **Isaiah 6:1-8**

Can you see the splendor that Isaiah saw? Can you grasp the magnitude of the scene that surrounds him? What does he feel? What is it about his experience that moves him to say, "Here am I, send me"?

This was an emotional experience, don't you think? His response must have been emotional, too, but it was far more. His commitment – his "here am I; send me" was a life-long commitment.

Meditate
> Is there anything or any one in your life that would keep you from saying, "Here am I; send me" to God?

Pray

_____

Here am I; send me.
Isaiah 6:8 (KJV)

_____

Notes

_____

_____

_____

> I encouraged you to begin this 40-day quest with the hope that it would affect your relationship with God. Has it? How about your relationships with other people?

Please Don't Make Me Go to Ohio!

I grew up on the High Plains of West Texas. I loved that flat land where you could see for miles in any direction. I loved the tumbleweeds and cotton farms and hot, dry days and cool nights of summer. Most of all, I loved the people—especially the people in Tahoka, the little town that gave me the opportunity to get started in full-time ministry. We lived there eight years during my 20's. It was the good life as far as I was concerned.

A letter from a pastor in Ohio threatened that good life. "Come over into Macedonia and help us," he wrote. His church made it official by calling me to a staff position.

That letter began an inner war: the lure of the good life in Tahoka fighting it out with that never-forgotten eleven year old boy's call to missions. Should I go? Should I stay? What did God want me to do?

One afternoon, I decided to pray in my office until I got an answer. I began by asking God what he wanted me to do, but

> Meditation for some religions is an attempt to empty the mind. Meditating on scripture is the opposite. It is filling your mind and heart with God's word. Don't hurry through the meditation time.

my praying gradually shifted to thinking about leaving West Texas. That was home. Ohio was a foreign country a long way from home. I thought of all that we would be leaving behind.

Finally, I cried out to God in one of the most sincere prayers of my life, "Oh, God! Please, don't make me go to Ohio!"

"Okay." It was as if God got up and left the room.

I don't think I have ever felt so alone, so empty. I realized that I had prayed a foolish prayer.

Seven years later, a merciful God gave me another chance. The same church called again. This time my response to God was, "Send me. I'll go."

We ministered in Ohio for 26 years. I consider that to be one of the greatest joys of my life. I almost missed it.

Weekly Reflection

You are continuing to add to your prayer vocabulary.
Take a few minutes to review the last seven.

Which prayer has had the most impact on
your relationship with God so far?

Have you found yourself using any of the prayers
in conversations with God throughout the day?

Have any of the prayers come on "just the right day?"
That will happen occasionally and leave you amazed at
God's timing

Has God revealed any area of your
life where you are not willing to say,
"Your will be done?"

Day 22   Date_____

Context
　A man whose son was possessed by an evil spirit brought his son to Jesus to heal him, "If you can." When Jesus said anything was possible if a person believed, the desperate man cried out, "Lord, I believe; help my unbelief."

Read
Mark 9: 14-29

Here is a man who dares to be honest with God.

Notice three parts of his appeal to Jesus:
1. He addressed Jesus as "Lord', a recognition of His sovereignty.
2. He believed Jesus could heal his son.
3. In case there were any lingering doubts, he asked Jesus to take those away.

Instead of bragging about the strength of his faith, he asked for help for the weakness of his faith. He did not see himself as a super saint, but as a believer with a sometimes imperfect or weak faith. He did not let his imperfect faith lead him to settle for less than a super-saint's faith. In humility he asked for more faith.

Meditate

Pray

Lord, I believe; help my unbelief.
Mark 9:24 (NKJV)

Notes

_____

_____

_____

_____

I Do Believe . . . Sort of

I have prayed this prayer more than any other prayer in the Bible.

I do believe. How could I not after all that God has allowed me to experience in the past 66 years that confirms His presence, that proves the truth of His Word, that shows beyond a doubt that He loves me?

Yet, sometimes a sliver of a doubt begins to slip out of some hidden spot in a deep recess in my mind. I try to ignore it; but it eludes my attempts at suppression and whispers, a little louder than before, "How do you know? Are you sure?"

The God who knows all about me, who knows about my questions that no one else hears, does not turn me away because of my questions. He knows my heart. He answers them.

He answers with a passage of scripture that I "just happen to come across". He answers it with a worship experience in which His presence is so real I can almost touch Him. He answers with a reminder from our history together. I imagine He has ways to answer that He hasn't used yet.

The God who knows all about me, who knows about my questions that no one else hears, does not turn me away because of my questions. He knows my heart.

My prayer does not surprise him. He understands that I am not the man of faith that some people tell me I am. I have fooled them, but not Him.

He knows my heart, my desire to believe, so He put this prayer in the Gospel so people like me – people whose minds ask questions others have long ago left behind, people whose memories of His past answers to this prayer need to be jogged. He put this prayer in the Bible so we could know that we can ask and He will answer again

I am awestruck once more by His love.

37

Day 23   Date_____

Context
    Moses had had it. He was up to here with the complaining
    ingrates he had been given to lead from slavery in Egypt to a
    new life in the Promised Land.

Read
Numbers 11: 1 - 30

You can read Moses' exhaustion in his words. He was almost at
the end of his rope. Notice that in this case, God's response to
Moses' request was immediate.

Do you have a "been there, done that" response to Moses'
weariness? If you are not there right now, you probably have vivid
memories of those times you were ready to throw in the towel.
And you realize that they will come again.

Meditate
    Do you always recognize when the load is too heavy or do
    you struggle with trying to do things on your own?
    How would constantly remembering "I can't, but God can"
    affect your life?

Pray

_____

**I can't carry all these people by myself!
The load is far too heavy.
Numbers 11:14 (NLT)**

_____

Notes

_____

_____

_____

_____

_____

Day 24   Date_____

Context
>   Jeremiah had faithfully preached God's message to His
>   people, but few listened. Disaster was coming. Jeremiah
>   reminds God that he stayed at the task and asked God to
>   stay with him. He had no other hope.

Read
>   **Jeremiah 17: 11-18**

If we live long enough most, if not all of us, will personally
experience one or more days of disaster. A friend asked an older
Christian how she had managed to get through some really
tough times over a 50-year period. Her answer: "You have to
know the promises."

In the first 23 days of this prayer journal, you have talked with the
Lord about several of His promises. This is a good time to re-visit
those with Him.

Meditate
>   Are there things or people you might be tempted to see as
>   your hope in place of God in a day of disaster?
>   Where will God be in any day of disaster you may face?

Pray

_____

LORD, do not desert me now!
You alone are my hope in the day of disaster.
Jeremiah 17:17 (NLT)

_____

Notes

_____

_____

_____

_____

_____

I'm Afraid

I was diagnosed with Parkinson's disease (PD) in 1996. PD is a chronic, progressive malfunctioning of the brain's messaging system that can result in varying degrees of tremor, slowness, stiffness, and clumsiness.

Routine activities such as getting up from of a chair, walking across a room, swallowing food, brushing one's teeth, buttoning a shirt, jotting down a telephone number, walking up and down stairs, and driving a car can be challenges for the person with Parkinson's. PD is called a movement disorder, but it has other effects as well. Depression, fatigue, urological difficulties, digestive problems, inability to handle stress, voice difficulties such as loss of volume and poor enunciation, chronic insomnia, declining cognitive abilities--all can be part of the disease.

Routine activities such as getting up from of a chair, walking across a room, swallowing food, brushing one's teeth, buttoning a shirt, jotting down a telephone number, walking up and down stairs can be challenges for a person with Parkinson's.

Doctors treat the symptoms of the disease with medication and surgery while researchers continue to search for a cure. I thank God for the medications—they make my life easier, but my neurologist says a cure is probably too late for me.

"Your Parkinson's is never going to get better. It is only going to get worse."

Most of the time I can handle all that I know about Parkinson's because of the hundreds of ways God has allowed me to experience His love. I am confident that He will continue to walk with me—at least most of the time I am confident. But sometimes that confidence is shaky. Sometimes I get frightened.

My wife and I belong to a Parkinson's support group. I see men there--men about my age who sit in wheel chairs; their heads slumped on their chest or on the table in front of them, unable to speak intelligibly. I tell myself that I will fight this thing with everything I have, that I will never end up like that . . . but lately it has hit me that I might.

That frightens me and I am reminded to turn to the Lord and admit I am scared. It helps to be able to tell Him that I am afraid.

40

Date_____

Context
> David had every reason to be afraid. A jealous King Saul was bent on killing him. He fled to the Philistines, Saul's long-time enemies, but quickly realized that he was not safe there either. He escaped by feigned insanity.

Read
> **I Samuel 21:10 -15; Psalm 56: 1-13**

Meditate
> What are you afraid of? Long-term? Short term?
> As an introduction to your meditation and prayer time, take a brief moment to jot down a few things that frighten you. After meditation and prayer, come back to your list in the light of your time with the Lord.

> I am afraid of
> 1. _____
>
> 2. _____
>
> 3. _____
>
> 4. _____
> Come back to your "fear list" occasionally to check on your faith progress.

Pray

_____

When I am afraid, I will trust in you.
Psalm 56:3 (NIV)

_____

Notes
_____

_____

_____

Day 26   Date_____

Context
   The introduction of Psalm 102 calls it "A prayer of an afflicted
   man. When he is faint and pours out a lament before the
   Lord." At one point he accuses God of taking him up and
   throwing him aside.

Read
   Psalm 9: 1-10

Meditate.
   Has God ever forsaken you? Have you ever felt that God had
   thrown you aside? You and I may feel that He has thrown us
   aside, but has He ever done that?

Pray

_____

You, LORD, have never forsaken those who seek you.
Psalm 9:10 (NIV)

_____

Notes

_____

_____

You probably find yourself recalling your time to *be still
and know* and the prayer of the day throughout the day.
Try this: hold off making notes about your experience
with the prayer until just before going to bed.
Advantages: (1) more time to experience the prayer of
the day throughout the day before you write, (2) puts a
perfect cap on the day. Disadvantage is you might not
make it back to your notes.

Context
A cry for relief from distress ends in the psalmist being able to lie down and sleep in peace because God is there.

Read
Psalm 4: 1- 8

My wife, Shirley, and I both lost our first spouses through death when we were in our early 30's. Shirley said that she did not go to bed for two weeks after her husband 's death. She was so afraid of the silence that she sat up reading or watching television until she fell asleep in a chair or on the couch.

Finally, one night she was totally exhausted and knew she had to go to bed and try to sleep. As she lay in the bed she prayed that God would take away the fear and loneliness and replace it with His presence. She was immediately overwhelmed with the presence of God physically and spiritually relaxing her body. She fell asleep and slept soundly.

Each day can bring its share of care and struggle; each night its potential for tossing and turning and sleeplessness, but we can lie down in peace and sleep knowing that God will keep us safe.

Meditate
Do you have the kind of peace that enables you to lie down in peace and sleep?

Pray

_____

**I will lie down and sleep in peace, for you alone, O LORD, make me dwell in safety.
Psalm 4:8 (NIV)**

_____

Notes
_____

_____

_____

Day 28   Date_____

Context
>   The disciples observed Jesus in prayer and asked Him to
>   teach them to pray. He taught them what is popularly called
>   "The Lord's Prayer".

Read
>   **Luke 11: 1-14**

Jesus said to ask God for our food day by day. (Food, in this case,
can symbolize all of our physical or fiscal needs.)

That does not mean that we should not plan ahead or that we
should foolishly waste the resources we have today, trusting Him
to replace them tomorrow. That is irresponsible.

We should do our best to be good financial managers, but our
trust should be in Him, not our portfolio. Our employer may go
bankrupt and take our retirement fund with him. We may
become disabled. A family member may have catastrophic
medical bills. The believer need not fear. We can pray, "Give us
our food day by day."

Meditate

Pray

_____

Give us day by day the food we need.
Luke 11:3 (TEV)

_____

Notes

_____

_____

_____

_____

_____

_____

44

Weekly Reflection

You are continuing to add to your prayer vocabulary.
Take a few minutes to review the last seven.

Which prayer has had the most impact on
your relationship with God so far?

Have you found yourself using any of the prayers
in conversations with God throughout the day?

Have any of the prayers come on "just the right day?"
That will happen occasionally and leave you amazed at
God's timing.

God answers my questions with a passage of scripture that I
"just happen to come across".
He answers it with a worship experience in which His
presence is so real I can almost touch Him.
He answers with a reminder from our history together.
I imagine He has ways to answer that He hasn't used yet.

One Day At A Time

The opportunity to serve almost a year as interim pastor of First Baptist Church in Perrysburg, Ohio convinced Shirley and me that God wanted us to change the direction of our ministry. He called me to preach after thirty years as a minister of music and youth. That meant more preparation. So we sold our house, loaded everything we could carry in a U-Haul and pointed the truck southwest toward Fort Worth, Texas to return to the seminary where we had met years earlier.

The encouragement of family and friends seemed to verify our own convictions that this was what God wanted us to do. As we said our good-by's in Ohio and began the long drive to Texas I did not have a doubt that we were following God's direction and that He would enable us to complete the assignment.

> Talking about what you are learning and experiencing will help you organize your thoughts and is a great memory device. Tell someone else. It can bless them, too.

Once we moved into student housing (at 50 years old) and I started classes, however, the reality hit that we had taken a big step.

I wanted God to show us on paper how we could make it financially all the way to graduation and keep our youngest daughter in college at the same time. It did not work that way. He provided for only one semester at a time. One semester, it was an interim pastorate while the church looked for a permanent pastor. Another semester, a professor asked me to be his grader – a position that paid a generous stipend. Two families from our church in Toledo assisted our daughter and me with tuition fees and living expenses. It took us 4 regular semesters and 3 full summers to graduate. God always provided a way, but He did not give us much advance notice.

We knew we were supposed to be there. God showed us one semester at a time how we could stay. It was an important lesson to learn.

Day 29   Date_____

Context
    Threatened by imminent attack by a large army, King
    Jehosphaphat of Judah leads his people in a national fast
    and then prays for God's direction.

Read
    2 Chronicles 20: 4-12

Are you facing a desperate situation for which you have no
solution? This is a good time to apply this scripture. Talk to God
about what is going on.
    - Review the situation with Him.
    - Tell Him you give up; you are turning to Him for a solution.
    - Be still. Rest in Him. Trust Him to show you what to do next.
    - Be sure to tell others what God has done when He does act.

Meditate
    Can you think of times when God got you out of an
    impossible situation, but you did not recognize it as His doing?
    Make a list of those times.

Pray

_____

We do not know what to do, but
our eyes are upon you.
2 Chronicles 20:12 (NIV)

_____

Notes

_____

_____

_____

_____

_____

_____

_____

Day 30   Date_____

Context
    A shepherd writes about his relationship with God in terms of his occupation, his every day life.

Read
    Psalm 23: 1-6

    How often do you think about death and about Heaven that waits for the believer on the other side of death?
    My pastor said recently that one sign that we are succumbing to a spirit of materialism is that we seldom think about heaven.
    Psalm 116:15 says, *Precious in the sight of the Lord is the death of His saints.*
    For some of us that day may be many years away; for some of us it may be soon. One thing is sure. We will not make that passage alone.

Meditate
    As you meditate and then pray Psalm 23:4 see how God uses this prayer as preparation for that day.

Pray

_____

**Even though I walk through the valley of the shadow of death I will fear no evil,
for you are with me.
Psalm 23:4 (NIV)**

_____

Notes

_____

_____

_____

Have you been praying for God to change your "want to"?

48

Day 31   Date_____

Context
   The psalmist knows God is always with Him.

Read
   Psalm 63: 1-11

Occasional insomnia is a nuisance. Chronic insomnia can be a serious health hazard. The remedies are varied and range from helpful, to ineffective, to harmful, to "you've got to be kidding". Take a sleeping pill, raid the refrigerator, turn on the TV, read a book, write a letter, count sheep (does anyone do that?), update your Blackberry, call one of those all-night talk shows, wake up your spouse and say, "Let's talk." (Not recommended).

David had a better idea in Psalm 63. He said as he lay in bed he remembered God. He thought of Him through the watches of the night. Through the watches of the night indicates he may have been awake for quite awhile.

The next time you have trouble sleeping, instead of letting "Oh, no, not again! I've got to get some sleep! Tomorrow is a busy day" panic add to your urgency to sleep, try a different approach.

Meditate.

Pray

_____

On my bed I remember you; I think of you through the watches of the night.
Psalm 63:6 (NIV)

_____

Notes

_____

_____

_____

_____

Day 32   Date_____

Context
> Today's model prayer is the first sentence in a psalm of praise. It is fitting that it begins with our recognizing that He should get all the glory for anything good that happens or that we accomplish.

Today's prayer can help us focus on where all the glory should go—to God—and free us from the need to have it go where it does not need to go—to us.

After the New England Patriots won their third Super Bowl in four years, a reporter asked someone who knows Patriots coach Bill Belichik what his strength is as a coach. The man replied, "He has no ego."

How different would churches be if individual Christians would consistently focus on Christ and His name being glorified while being unconcerned about getting any credit for themselves?

Read
> **Psalm 115: 1-18**

Meditate
> The first sentence of day 1 in Rick Warren's 40-day study of *The Purpose Driven Life* is "It is not about you."
> Paul said in Philippians that it did not matter if some jealous preachers were making him look bad. They were proclaiming the Gospel and that is what matters.

Pray

Not to us, O LORD, not to us, but to your name be the glory. Psalm 115:1 (NIV)

Notes

_____

_____

_____

Day 33   Date_____

Context

I first heard of this prayer in a sermon at the Southern Baptist Pastors Conference in Norfolk, VA in 1976. I began praying it. It was one of the first borrowed prayers that I adopted for my own use. I have prayed it almost on a daily basis ever since. God has answered it often.

Read
I Chronicles 4: 9-10

This could be a selfish prayer, but it is not selfish to pray it this way:
Oh, that you would bless me indeed - Father, I want all You have to offer as far as a relationship with You is concerned. I crave that blessing.
Enlarge my territory – Give me more opportunities to share these blessing with others.
That Your hand would be with me – I know I can have little impact for the Kingdom on my own, but with Your hand upon me, I can touch others for Christ.
Keep me from sin, that I may not cause pain – Father, don't let me hurt others through my sin.

Meditate

Pray

_____

Oh that You would bless me indeed and enlarge my territory. That Your hand would be with me and that you would keep me from sin that I might not cause pain.
I Chronicles 4:9-10 (paraphrased)

_____

Notes

_____

_____

_____

Day 34   Date_____

    God assures us of His sovereignty, and then says He wants us
    to trust Him.

Read
    Psalm 50: 1-15

Sooner or later, most of us will experience tough times that go
beyond every day life. You will experience losses and set backs
that may dominate your life for a few days or for a few years. You
may feel that you have reached the limit of your endurance. You
may question where God is in all this.

He will be where He has always been: beside us. Psalm 50:15
says He wants us to trust Him so that He can rescue us and we
can give Him the glory.

Let your meditation today be similar to Day 1 when most of your
time was spent listening.

Meditate
    Is there a special area where God wants you to trust Him?
    Listen.

Pray

              _____

I want you to trust me in your times of trouble, so that I can rescue you and you can give me the glory. Psalm 50:15 (TLB)

              _____

Notes

_____

_____

_____

_____

_____

Oh, God, Please Help Me!

Her name was Nettie. She was a quiet, gentle, loving person whom I adored. We married while we were in college, expecting to live happily ever after.

We did. For thirteen years. Then Nettie died.

She was 33 years old, waiting for a kidney transplant.

I did not handle her death well. A week after she died I reasoned that if she were alive she would be suffering as she had for six years. Now she was in Heaven. She was not suffering. If I really loved her, I told myself, I would be happy for her. Grief was just selfishness on my part. God had given me the wonderful gift of being married to her for thirteen years. How could I complain now?

That kind of unrealistic thinking led to even greater heartache in the long run. Since I did not allow myself to grieve I turned to starting a new life. I began dating far too early, looking for someone to fill that awful loneliness in my heart. My family and Nettie's family were hurt, my friends horrified, my daughters confused, and my church alarmed by what some thought was scandalous behavior.

There were times when grief forced its way in, but my solution was to grit my teeth, swallow hard, and try to ignore it.

Two years went by. One day I was in my office at the church when something reminded me of Nettie. This time instead of trying to fight off the grief I ran next door to a house the church used for classrooms. No one was there. I fell on my knees and began sobbing like a baby. Finally, I cried out, "Oh, God, please help me."

Instantly, there was peace. It was as if God put His arms around me, assuring me that He had been there all the time. I began to thumb through the Psalms in the *Living Bible*. I came to Psalm 50:15, which on that day seemed to have been put there just for me.

God said, "I want you to trust Me in your time of trouble so I can rescue you and you can give me the glory."

The darkness of the last two years began to turn to light.

Day 35   Date_____

Context

The authorities told the apostles that if they did not stop
preaching about Jesus there would be severe consequences.
And those were not empty threats. The officials who made
them could also see to it that those threats were carried out.

So what did the apostles do? They prayed for God to give them
the boldness to keep on doing the very thing that had gotten
them into trouble in the first place. And God answered their
prayers and they got into more trouble just as promised. But they
turned the world upside down.

Read
Acts 4:13-31

This was not the prayer of "Super Saints". The Bible teaches that
these were people just like you and me. (See James 5:17). It was
God who enabled them to be bold. How do you think He will
answer if you borrow their prayer?

Meditate

Pray

Enable your servants to speak your word with great boldness.
Acts 4:29 (NIV)

Notes

_____

_____

_____

_____

_____

_____

54

Weekly Reflection

You are continuing to add to your prayer vocabulary.
Take a few minutes to review the last seven.

Which prayer has had the most impact on
your relationship with God so far?

Have you found yourself using any of the prayers
in conversations with God throughout the day?

Have any of the prayers come on "just the right day?"
That will happen occasionally and leave you amazed at
God's timing.

Are you facing a desperate situation for which you have no
solution? This is a good time to pray, "We don't know what
to do but our eyes are upon you." (2 Chronicles 20:12)
Talk to God about what is going on.
Review the situation with Him.
Tell Him you give up; you are turning to Him for a solution.
Be still.
Rest in Him.
Trust Him to show you what to do next.
Be sure to tell others what God has done when He does act.

Years ago a friend gave me a book on salesmanship that insisted that a salesman should always take time before talking to a potential customer to assess that person's needs and then honestly ask how he could help that person. Let's adapt that habit regarding any time we need to enlist someone or face any issues with them. Always breathe a prayer, asking God to grant you success with the person you are about to speak with.

Context
> Nehemiah was a Jewish exile who held a high position in the government of the Persian Empire. He longed to return to Jerusalem to help rebuild the walls of the destroyed city. He needed the permission and the support of the pagan king. He asked God to give him success when he asked the king.

Read
> **Nehemiah 1:1-2:8**

Meditate

Pray

Give your servant success today by granting (me) favor in the presence of this man.
Nehemiah 1:11 (NIV)

Notes

_____

_____

_____

_____

_____

_____

_____

Day 37   Date_____

Context
The great missionary, Paul, had been struggling with an
insurmountable difficulty and he asked God to take it away.
God said, "No."

Read
2 Corinthians 12:1-10

This truth is the opposite of the untruths the "health and wealth"
preachers spread via television. Paul walked as closely with God
as anyone in the Bible, yet he suffered with some problem that
God would not take away.

Why? See if you can find the answer as you read, meditate, pray,
and write about it.

Meditate

Pray

_____

My grace is sufficient for you,
for my power is made perfect in weakness.
2 Corinthians 12:9 (NIV)

_____

Notes

_____

_____

_____

_____

_____

_____

_____

_____

_____

What If Weakness Is All I Have Left?

--Journal Entry, May 31, 2005

God spoke to me in the Sunday morning worship at Christ Chapel Bible Church. He did it through something my neurologist said two years ago, a scripture I have thought about over and over lately, and a sermon by Darril Holden. He tied the three together to give me another glimpse of how He is working out Romans 8:28 in my life.

Two years ago Dr.Shank, told me that my Parkinson's was never going to get better; it would only get worse. She said even if a cure were discovered tomorrow, it was too late for me.

I know that is true, but that does not mean I should sit down and accept the inevitable. God did not make me that way. No, I see this as a race—the race of my life—a race to stay one step ahead of the Parkinson's disease for as long as I can. I am still in the lead, but I can feel Parkinson's nipping at my heels. God put me in this race and He has not said anything about quitting.

Ninety percent of the time I feel fine. I usually go four or five months at a time when I am able to function almost normally—as long as I keep popping those prescriptions every 4 to 4 ½ hours.

Then comes the inevitable crash.

The latest hit Saturday, May 21.

It has been a tough ten days since. I have had repeated incidents of freezing—the phenomena where to initiate movement I have to literally think, "Move your foot". Then, when my feet do start to move, I have to concentrate to take a full stride. Otherwise, my gait is a shuffle of short, choppy steps. I have always been a high-energy person, but now fatigue catches me off guard with both its suddenness and its severity. Speech problems that were bad enough when my primary concerns were volume and enunciation now include the more serious struggle of what to say. My thinking seems slow and confused when my mouth is moving, embarrassing me and making me hesitant to speak at all. Last week, I finally faced the possibility that, like other Parkinson's people, I may eventually lose the ability to speak. That is a tough one to deal with.

And the timing of this flare up of PD coincided with the beginning of the Cats season. My work with Baseball Chapel shifted into a higher gear and my weaknesses seemed more pronounced than ever.

Sunday morning I kept thinking about all this in light of 2 Corinthians 12:8-10. Lately, I have thought about that scripture often. I keep coming back to its assurance that God can use my weaknesses as His strength.

Then it hit me. I have always wanted to serve God from my strengths—strong voice, articulate speech, discipline, preparation, doing everything to the best of my ability. Now all that is gone.

Weakness is all I have left to give Him.

Seconds later, Darril Holden began introducing his sermon about Jacob wrestling with God. Darril said Jacob had fought all his life. He won when he finally gave up. I sat there amazed again at God's timing. I have no doubt that He led me to process all that about my weakness as a prelude to Darril's sermon.

Later, Darril said, "The most significant moment in your life will be when you finally stop struggling with God and start clinging to Him."

Thank You, Lord. You are not through with me yet, are you?

Day 38   Date_____

The Apostle John writes a description of a worship scene in heaven.

"Worship is not a spectator sport" was the title of one of my earliest sermons. I was trying to make the point that worship is God-centered. True worshippers are active participants, not spectators. How do you evaluate worship? Do you evaluate how effective it was by how much you got out of it? How moving it was? How beautiful the music or how powerful the sermon? True worship is about God, not us.

Read
Revelation 4: 1- 11

Allow your mind's eye to see this scene in heaven as best you can. It is a scene that is beyond our comprehension and will be until we experience it someday ourselves. As you meditate on today's prayer and begin to pray it to Him as part of your ongoing prayer vocabulary, it will be interesting to see what impact it will have on your participation in future worship services.

Meditate

Pray

Holy, Holy, Holy...Lord, God Almighty, who was, and is, and is to come. Revelation 4:8 (NIV)

Notes

_____

_____

_____

_____

_____

Date_____

I sometimes use this verse with a little humor, intentionally misquoting to say, "Shirley, goodness and mercy shall follow me all the days of my life".

Laying humor aside, it is not being disrespectable to use this psalm to be reminded of the incredible gift of love He gave 30 years ago when Shirley became my wife. She is the most giving, loving person I have ever known—and I get to experience her for the rest of my life.

Of course, as wonderful as Shirley is, she does not come close to the love God keeps on giving me. This psalm becomes a vehicle to celebrate my relationship with God that will last for eternity.

Context
    Psalm 23 is probably the best-known psalm to the average person. It uses the picture of a Palestinian shepherd taking care of his sheep to help us understand God taking care of us.

Read
    Psalm 23:1-8

Meditate
    Consider how God is acting as your shepherd even now.

Pray

_____

Surely Your goodness and mercy will follow me all the days of my life and I will live in Your house forever. Psalm 23:8 (personalized from KJV)

_____

Notes

_____

_____

_____

Hiding From the Hurricane
--Journal Entry, Wed, Sept 21, 2005

Another hurricane is brewing hundreds of miles out in the Gulf of Mexico. The weather professionals are watching it, measuring it, plotting its course. With the Gulf Coast still reeling from the devastation of Hurricane Katrina, this new storm—Rita by name—may slam its way ashore by the weekend.

God seems to have used all the attention we are focusing on these storms to help me understand my relationship with Him.

It is far too much hyperbole to compare my situation with the disruption Hurricane Katrina has caused thousands of people, yet God seems to be using all the attention we are focusing on these storms to help me better understand my relationship with Him.

I woke up earlier than I intended this morning, but I welcomed the extra time that might be just what I needed to finish writing the prayer journal. I have gone to bed other nights thinking tomorrow would be that day, but each tomorrow has brought more delays, more changes, more exasperation. My old type-A personality kicks in, my blood pressure rises dangerously, I feel out-of-control, the wrap-up day never arrives.

Putting the prayer journal together has become an unbelievable grind. I have told my family that either God does not want me to publish this or I am under attack by the enemy who does not want people to be encouraged to *be still and know*.

I have not handled the situation well and the enemy has used that to taunt me, pointing out the hypocrisy of writing about *being still before God* in a state of sustained tension that has marked my days lately. When I have disobeyed God the enemy has cackled in my ear about the gall of one who rebels against God after telling other people how to deal with sin in their heart.

That is how it was this morning when I opened my Bible at the place I stopped yesterday, the end of Psalm 56. My eyes moved to Psalm 57 and I began to read the passage for today. It could not have been more timely. I could hardly catch my breath as I read.

Have mercy on me, O God, have mercy!
I look to you for protection. I will hide beneath the shadow of
your wings until this violent storm is past Ps. 57:1 (NLT)

The hurricane pounding toward the Texas coast at this moment is a picture of the enemy storming my heart, but I am safe. Like a chick scurrying to the safety of its mother's wings, I can find security, protection, and peace–all that I need under God's wings. From the safety of that place I can see the truth.

I had deluded myself into thinking that the writer of a book like this has to be a Super-Saint—a flawless example of what I am writing about. I had it half right. I can set an example, but it is not the example I intended. It is the example of a Not-So-Super Saint who, like that frightened chick, has run for the protection of God's wings and found safety there. Come and join me.

Day 40   Date_____

Context
   The inscription that precedes this psalm in the Bible is a psalm
   of David regarding the time he fled from Saul and went into
   the cave.

Read
   Psalm 57:1- 11

Meditate

Pray

_____

I will hide beneath the shadow of your wings
until this violent storm is past.
Psalm 57:1 (NLT)

_____

Notes

_____

_____

_____

_____

_____

_____

_____

_____

_____

_____

_____

_____

_____

Forty Borrowed Prayers

Day 1 Be still, and know that I am God - Psalm 46:10 (NIV)

Day 2 Who are you, Lord? - Acts 26:15 (NIV)

Day 3 You will seek me and find me when you seek me with all your heart - Jeremiah 29:13 (NIV)

Day 4 God be merciful to me a sinner - Luke 18:13 (KJV)

Day 5 My Lord and my God. - John 20:28. (KJV)

Day 6 My heart has heard you say, "Come and talk with me." And my heart responds, "LORD, I am coming." - Psalm 27:8 (NLT)

Day 7 You are the God who sees me. - Genesis 16:13 (NIV)

Day 8 Lord, teach us to pray. - Luke 11:1 (NIV)

Day 9 I am filled with awe by the amazing things you have done. - Habakkuk 3:2 (NLT)

Day 10 Father, hallowed be your name. - Luke 11:2 (NIV)

Day 11 Search me, O God, and know my heart: try me, and know my thoughts: and see if there be any wicked way in me. - Psalm 139:23-24 (KJV)

Day 12 Have mercy upon me, O God, according to your loving kindness. - Psalm 51:1 (NKJV)

Day 13 Guide my steps by your word, so I will not be overcome by any evil. - Psalm 119:133 (NLT)

Day 14 (Praying for others) May _____ be filled with the knowledge of your will through all spiritual wisdom and understanding.
- personalized paraphrase of Colossians 1:9 (NIV)

Day 15 Forgive us our sins--just as we forgive those who have sinned against us. - Luke11:4 (NLT)

Day 16 Your kingdom come, your will be done - Matthew 6:10 (NIV)

Day 17 Not my will, but thine, be done. - Luke 22:42 (KJV)

Day 18 Create in me a clean heart, O God. - Psalm 51:10 (KJV)

Day 19 Don't let us yield to temptation. - Luke 11:4 (NLT)

Day 20 Speak, LORD, your servant is listening. - 1 Samuel 3:9 (NIV)

Day 21 Here am I; send me. - Isaiah 6:8 (KJV)

Day 22 Lord, I believe; help my unbelief! - Mark 9:24 (NKJV)

Day 23 I can't carry all these people by myself! The load is far too heavy - Numbers 11:14 (NLT)

Day 24 LORD, do not desert me now! You alone are my hope in the day of disaster. - Jeremiah 17:17 (NLT)

Day 25 When I am afraid, I will trust in you. - Psalm 56:3 (NIV)

Day 26 You, LORD, have never forsaken those who seek you. - Psalm 9:10 (NIV)

Day 27 I will lie down and sleep in peace, for you alone, O LORD, make me dwell in safety. - Psalm 4:8 (NIV)

Day 28 Give us day by day the food we need. - Luke 11:3 (TEV)

Day 29 We do not know what to do, but our eyes are upon you. - 2 Chronicles 20:12 (NIV)

Day 30 Even though I walk through the valley of the shadow of death, I will fear no evil, for you are with me. -Psalm 23:4 (NIV)

Day 31 On my bed I remember you; I think of you through the watches of the night. - Psalm 63:6 (NIV)

Day 32 Not to us, O LORD, not to us but to your name be the glory. Psalm 115:1 (NIV)

Day 33 Oh, that You would bless me indeed and enlarge my territory. That Your hand would be with me and that you would keep me from sin that I might not cause pain.
 - paraphrase of 1 Chronicles 4:9-10

Day 34 I want you to trust me in your times of trouble, so that I can rescue you and you can give me the glory. - Psalm 50:15 (TLB)

Day 35 Enable your servants to speak your word with great boldness. - Acts 4:29 (NIV)

Day 36 Give your servant success today by granting (me) favor in the presence of this man. - Nehemiah 1:11 (NIV)

Day 37 My grace is sufficient for you, for my power is made perfect in weakness . - 2 Corinthians 12:9 (NIV)

Day 38 Holy, holy, holy...Lord, God Almighty, who was, and is, and is to come. - Revelation 4:8 (NIV)

Day 39 Surely, Your goodness and mercy will follow me all the days of my life, and I will live in your house forever.
 - Psalm 23:6 (personalized from KJV)

Day 40 I will hide beneath the shadow of your wings until this violent storm is past. - Psalm 57:1 (NLT)

Meaningful Meditation
Beats the Boring Kind

One man described meditation as sitting very still, looking at a spot on the floor, breathing slowly, listening to your breathing, and thinking about nothing—and this was by a writer trying to convince us to meditate!

Meditation to empty the mind plays a major role in eastern religions. Transcendental Meditation (TM), popular in the United States in the 1970's, and yoga, touted by some fitness gurus today, both teach using meditation leading to emptiness.

Sounds boring to me. Biblical meditation is far more attractive. Instead of the emptiness or the meaningless boredom of eastern meditation the Bible talks about the blessings that come to the person who delights in God's word and who meditates on it night and day.

Biblical meditation engages the mind in unhurried thinking about the scripture, talking with God about what the scripture means, asking Him what He wants us to learn from it, how He wants us to use it.

Biblical meditation is honest about the context of the passage, being careful not to take a passage out of its context and force meaning into it that was never intended.

Biblical meditation and hurry do not go together. Always meditate in a relaxed spirit.

Eastern meditation uses a word or phrase, called a mantra, repeated over and over trying to reach mindlessness. One can meditate on one word from scripture, but the goal is always to mine it for its meaning and its message.

Meditating on the scriptures you are adding to your prayer vocabulary is a key part of this prayer journal. Don't cheat yourself by shorting your meditation time. If you do not normally meditate on scripture you may need to ask God to teach you.

You may find the line between prayer and meditation blurred after a while. That is okay. The more time you spend in prayer and meditation the more they will tend to merge, leading to some rich moments with God.

Confessions Of A Slow Learner

While the description of those early mornings in our living room in Toledo may seem idyllic, that daily time alone with God was a long time in coming. I am often a slow learner, far from being a spiritual giant when it comes to the things of God. The time that I have treasured for years as the best time of the day came after many fits and starts. It was not even something I wanted to do. It came from a sense of "I ought to". That pushed me to some "I did it" mornings interspersed with about as many "I should have" mornings that put me on a guilt trip to the next "I ought to" pledge to try it again.

I am often a slow learner, far from being a spiritual giant when it comes to the things of God. The time that I have treasured for years as the best time of the day came after many fits and starts.

I had been a habitual early riser since I began helping my dad on his milk route when I was in junior high school. A high school paper route required getting up at 5:00 a.m. and for awhile in college I worked the 4:30 to 8:30 a.m. shift as a clerk at the United States Post Office.

My first full-time church staff position was in Tahoka, Texas, a small town of 3,500 people. It was an agricultural community where the farmers got up early and I soon learned that Al's cafeteria was a bustling place at 6:00 a.m. I often joined the crowd there for coffee, politics, and the latest arguments about whether or not Craig Morton should replace Don Meredith as the Dallas Cowboys' quarterback.

It was not unusual for me to be in my office at the church even before that. I was finishing my college degree and if I had a paper to write, I preferred an early morning fresh start at the typewriter in the church office instead of burning the midnight oil.

On days I did not have a paper to write, I would often go by the office for another attempt at having a meaningful time of prayer. All those sermons about early morning prayer kept honing that sense of "I ought to".

I tried setting time goals to get my prayer time on track. I determined that I should spend so many minutes in prayer every day. I would look at the clock and dutifully begin. After praying for a long I time, I would glance at my watch only to discover that time moves slower during early morning prayer than at other times of the day. Constant glancing at my watch did not add to the wonder of spending time with God.

My mind would wander off in many directions. I wrote a prayer list to help me focus, only to find the list gave my mind more places to wander. Something was missing. There were occasional high moments when God seemed to speak to me in those prayer times or when I sensed that my prayers were getting through.

More often than not, however, that early morning time with Him did not come close to measuring up to the special time I heard other Christians talk about. I was not on their level spiritually.

I knew I should be, but frankly, I was not sure I really wanted to be. The sermons and the testimonies and the scriptures about prayer kept me coming back to try again. The combination of self-discipline and guilt when I did not spend that time in prayer finally pushed that "ought to" into a habit. A loving and patient God used that habit to lead me to enough meaningful experiences that the time alone with Him became a precious time of fellowship I did not want to miss. I began to look forward to that time with anticipation instead of dread. It took awhile, but my "ought to" had become a "get to."

By the time I was enjoying those mornings with Him in our home in Toledo I had been experiencing the "get to" phase for several years. I was thankful for that.

When is the best time for your quiet time with God? I am partial to early morning. Even if you are not a morning person, there is less likelihood of scheduling conflicts early in the morning. There are pros and cons for any time as your daily reserved time, but there is one time that is better than any other: the time you will do it.

70

Be Still in a Small Group

Sharing, Encouraging, and Accountability in a Small Group

This prayer journal is based on spending time alone with God every day. We need that quiet time, that intimacy between just the two of us, but we also need other believers. God made us that way.

Going through the forty days at the same time as others in a small group and meeting regularly with them to share your experiences should make it even more meaningful for all of you. You will treasure the sharing, encouraging, and accountability that group members will offer each other.

A Simple Plan for Small Groups

1. Meet weekly if possible
2. Keep it simple.
3. Enjoy being together.
4. Discuss the questions in the "Weekly Reflection" pages.
5. Pray together.
6. Agree to pray for each other throughout the week.

Learning to Pray as a Small Group

Among my fondest memories of Gateway Community Church is how we learned to pray together. One of our members said we needed to get everyone together just to pray—no other agenda, just pray. So, we did. About a dozen people met in our apartment on a Sunday night. I had never been in a prayer meeting quite like the one we had that night.

No one taught us how to pray together. We did not figure it out. Some might say it just happened. I prefer another explanation: God showed us. It became the pattern for the way we prayed after that.

There was no plan, no agenda, no prayer requests. We just bowed our heads and, as a group we were still before the Lord. No one prayed aloud for quite some time. We were all bonded together in prayer. The silence was comfortable.

After awhile someone spoke aloud to God. They spoke from their heart in every day language. More silence followed. There was no rush. We were sitting quietly, part of God 's church loving Him, loving each other, and listening to Him.

We did not look at our watches. Someone read a passage of scripture they thought God wanted us to think about. Someone else spoke to the group about something on their heart. More spoken prayers. More silence. More reading of scripture that came to someone's mind. We did not "pray around the circle". Some prayed aloud several times, some not at all.

Finally, we said, "Amen". We knew something special had taken place that night, something we needed to continue. Praying like that in a small group became part of who we were, the DNA of Gateway Community Church.

We learned to make decisions as a church in prayer meetings like that. We did not vote. We prayed until there was unity—even if it meant postponing a decision to another time. I thank God every time I remember those prayer meetings and those special people.

It would be a mistake for a group to try to duplicate another group's prayer meetings, but you can sit down together, be still before the Lord with an unhurried heart, and as a group ask, "Lord, teach us to pray."

Then watch to see what happens.

Do You Want to Continue as a Not-So-Super Saint?

I used the term "Not-So-Super-Saint" in the title as <u>identification</u>, not as a <u>goal</u>. The term was meant to describe how I see myself and the believers I had in mind as I wrote the prayer journal. It was not meant as an excuse or permission for any of us to settle for less than God's best for us.

God Initiated This Relationship

We did not seek out God. He came looking for us. The cross proves that. In return He wants all of us—that is what He meant when He said we were to take up our cross and follow Him. That cross opens the door wide to an intimate relationship with Him. That relationship is the greatest gift He can give us.

Forty Days That Keep on Going

Has your time to be still with God become a habit that you will continue? Has your "ought to" become a "get to", a daily time you anticipate with delight? Pray that God will make that a reality. Pray that the forty days will be only the beginning. If you haven't started doing it already, start marking prayers you find as you read the Bible and develop your own list of prayers to borrow.

Do You Want Everything He Has to Offer?

The prayer that we borrowed from Jabez can lead us to desire every spiritual blessing He has. That being the case, will you come along with me in asking Him for everything He has to offer us, to desire the closest possible relationship with Him?

To Be More Like Jesus

His very nature is such that the closest possible relationship will lead us to become more and more like Him. That means we will not cling selfishly to these blessings, but eagerly look for ways to share them with others.

Order More Books?

Additional copies of *Shhh...Be Still and Know* are available for $10 (tax and shipping not included). To order, please email hollars@sbcglobal.net or call (817) 346-1387.

Please be sure to include name, address and telephone number, and allow two weeks for delivery.